Fun Backyard Bird Facts for Kids

Jacquelyn Elnor Johnson

www.CrimsonHillBooks.com

First edition, May 2022.

Cataloguing in Publication Data

Johnson, Jacquelyn Elnor

Fun Backyard Bird Facts for Kids

Description: Crimson Hill Books trade paperback edition | Nova Scotia, Canada

ISBN:	978-1-990887-00-0 (Paperback - Ingram)
BISAC:	JNF003030 Juvenile Nonfiction: Animals - Birds JNF016000 Juvenile Nonfiction: Curiosities & Wonders JNF048000 Juvenile Nonfiction: Reference - General
THEMA:	WNCB - Wildlife - Birds and birdwatching - General interest YNG - Children's - Teenage general interest - General knowledge and interesting facts YNNK - Children's - Teenage general interest - Birds

Record available at https://www.bac-lac.gc.ca/eng/Pages/home.aspx

Book design: Jesse Johnson

Crimson Hill Books
(a division of)
Crimson Hill Products Inc.
Lawrencetown, Nova Scotia
Canada

Crimson Hill
Books

Sparrows have come to this backyard to enjoy some peanuts. There are more Sparrows in the world than any other type of wild bird.

Most female birds don't sing, but female Cardinals do, especially when they're sitting on their nests. Female Cardinals sing a softer version of their mate's song.

Do you know backyard birds?

Right there, at the feeder. Do you see it? It grabs a single seed and darts away. It's a bird you might have seen before, or maybe not. Then you wonder, what kind of bird is it?

Birds live with us and among us, sharing our world, or we share their world. This has always been true. Even when you don't notice, birds are building their nests, having their babies and singing their songs. When they like what's on offer, they visit our gardens and feeders.

They're backyard birds.

It brings us joy to see them and hear their songs. They're colorful and fun to watch.

You probably already recognize some of them by name. They're the Robins, Wrens, Sparrows and Crows, and possibly you know the names of some others. But what is that little yellow bird you've just spotted? Or the one with the long pointy beak?

This book is about wild birds that choose to live near humans in North America. That's United States, Mexico and Canada. It's about the amazing facts and secret lives of the most common birds that are as close as our own backyards.

Backyard Bird Fun Fact:
Many birds eat small stones. They do this to help digest their food. Some of the dinosaurs did the same thing, millions of years ago.

Male Cardinals look after their mates and can be fierce in protecting their territories.

Northern Cardinal

You might think, from this bird's name, that it lives only way up North. Not true! Northern Cardinals live in the eastern half of United States and in the Southwest, almost all of Mexico and also in Southeastern Canada. They are the most common bird in Texas. "Common" means the bird you are mostly likely to see everywhere, including in your backyard.

All songbirds have amazing singing skills. In just one-tenth of a second, Northern Cardinals can race through all the notes on a piano – and more than that!

They can easily switch back and forth between the two sides of their syrinx without even taking a breath!

The syrinx is in their neck. It's what they use to make sounds, like humans use our larynx, or voice box.

Only the males are brilliantly red. Females are a soft sand brown. Their eggs can be pale blue or pale green with brown, purple and gray flecks. They like seeds, nuts and berries, but are wary of coming to feeders that are close to a house or building. Their usual food is insects.

If you hear a backyard bird calling sweet-sweet-sweet or cheer-cheer-cheer, it's a Northern Cardinal.

Cardinals are known for a strange bird practice called "anting." They allow ants to crawl all over their bodies. They might put some dead ants under their feathers. We're not sure why they do this, but it might be because formic acid from ants' bodies can kill lice. It might be the birds are using one insect to get rid of another, peskier insect. When Cardinals, and some other birds, can't find ants for anting, they use beetles, coffee grounds and even cigarette butts!

Sparrow

Sparrows are the most common wild bird in the world. They aren't a native bird in North America. They were brought from Europe to Brooklyn, New York in 1851. Back then, it seemed like a great idea! The Sparrows would eat all the Linden Moth caterpillars that were attacking the basswood trees in that city. This plan worked, but the Sparrows also thrived in their new home and there were soon so many of them, they spread out. In just 50 years, they were everywhere in United States, and beyond to Canada and Mexico.

Sparrows are immigrant birds, not native to North America, but they've been very successful settlers here!

Some native species of birds, like Eastern and Western Bluebirds, Orioles and some cliff-dwelling birds are being pushed out of their territories and now there are fewer of them because of Sparrows.

Today, there are many types of Sparrows in North America. Sparrows live almost everywhere in Canada and in all of United States except for Alaska and the furthest South. They like seeds and are happy to find them at feeders.

There are many types of Sparrows in North America, but they all look almost alike. There are the American Tree Sparrow, House Sparrow, Song Sparrow, Fox Sparrow and White-Throated Sparrow. The White-Throated Sparrow has the most unusual song, a high whistle that sounds like, "Old Sam Peabody, Peabody, Peabody."

Songbirds aren't born already knowing their songs, just like kids aren't born already knowing how to talk. All young creatures need to learn to do the things adults do. Sparrows are a songbird. Babies listen to the songs of their fathers and all the other male birds in nearby nests before they start to practice singing. At first, they aren't very good at it, but they keep trying. It's their instinct to learn their songs. Male Sparrows that can't sing the correct songs and the correct types of songs won't be able to attract a mate or keep their territory.

Sparrows prefer to live near people. They live in flocks, never alone. They eat seeds all year and insects in summer.

Blue Jay

Like all their Corvid cousins, Blue Jays are brilliant mimics. Corvids are a group of smart birds, including Crows, Ravens, Rooks, Nutcrackers, Jackdaws, Choughs, Treepies, Magpies, all types of Jays and Mockingbirds. There are no Choughs, Treepies, Rooks or Jackdaws in North America.

Blue Jays live in almost all of Southern Canada, Eastern and Central United States and Northeastern Mexico. They are rarely seen in Northwest United States. There are none in Alaska. Only some of them migrate before winter, mostly to Southern United States.

Backyard Bird Fun Fact:
Ravens cluck like hens when they detect danger.

Female and male Blue Jays look the same except females are a bit smaller. This is a male.

Wild Blue Jays and also ones that ornithologists have captured to study have shown that they know how to make tools from sticks or scraps of paper to get food. When other Blue Jays see this, they copy the same method.

In summer they eat insects, spiders and even small frogs along with acorns, tree nuts, seeds, berries and other fruits. A surprising thing about Blue Jays is they aren't actually blue. Their feathers are brown, but they reflect blue light, making them appear to be blue to humans. Birds have different vision than humans. They can see ultra-violet light which we can't see. They can also see colors we can't see and have no names for.

Blue Jays are helping the forests, especially oak trees. They bury so many acorns in their caches they sometimes forget where their acorns are. In this way, they're planting trees and helping to save the forests!

They're happy to find seeds and berries at feeders and especially like peanuts. Unlike most other backyard birds, Blue Jays are large enough and strong enough to crack open the shells, holding them firmly with their feet.

Blue Jays can be feeder bullies. To give the smaller birds a chance, have different types of feeders. Little birds prefer the small box-shaped or tube feeders, while bigger birds like Blue Jays would rather have a tray or platform feeder.

Nuthatch

Nuthatches are the dapper little gray, white and black birds you might spot hanging upside-down from your feeders, looking for seeds. There are two types, the Red-breasted Nuthatch, with an orangey-red neck and belly and the White-breasted, almost the same with a white throat and belly.

The Red-Breasted Nuthatch lives everywhere in United States except Florida and almost everywhere in Canada except the Far North. The White-breasted Nuthatch lives in Southern Canada and the Maritime provinces, all of United States except Alaska and Florida and central Mexico.

The White-breasted Nuthatch and the Red-breasted Nuthatch look almost alike.

Both types like insects and seeds. Red-breasted Nuthatches are known for stealing nest-building materials from other birds. White-breasted Nuthatches like to grab sunflower seeds and suet from feeders and hide it in tree bark to enjoy later.

Yellow-rumped Warbler

Warblers are songbirds with a trilling song. The Yellow-rumped Warbler is a master at eating insects. It can catch them mid-air or skim them off the surface of lakes or the ocean.

In Autumn, they switch to eating berries. Yellow-rumped Warblers spend their summers nesting and

Backyard Bird Fun Fact:
In one day, a Hummingbird needs to eat twice its own bodyweight. They have the highest metabolism of any bird. Metabolism means how fast your body is working.

Yellow-rumped Warblers live almost everywhere in North America.

having their families in Alaska, parts of the Western United States and almost everywhere in Canada. As the weather gets colder, they migrate to Southern United States, Mexico, Cuba and Central America.

They especially like raisins, suet and peanut butter.

Northern Mockingbird

Does it sound like there's a crowd of birds singing in your backyard, but you look and can't see a single one? If so, chances are you've got a Northern Mockingbird out there somewhere. They like to sing when they're hidden at the center of a thick shrub or tree.

This Northern Mockingbird was spotted in a Florida backyard.

Mockingbirds got their name because they're clever mimics. They can learn and remember hundreds of different songs and calls! They often fool people who hear them, imitating other birds' calls, music, car alarms, frogs' croaking, crickets chirping or any other sounds they like. They aren't total copycats, though. They also sing some songs of their own.

Northern Mockingbirds are one of the most common birds in United States. They are rare in Canada and they prefer to remain hidden, so they are seldom seen in backyards.

Backyard Bird Fun Fact:
Hummingbirds don't sing. The humming noise they make is their wings flapping.

Redpolls' superpower is surviving in very cold weather.

Common Redpoll

Redpolls look like sparrows, but with a small splash of color. The Common Redpoll has a red cap and a pinkish splash across their neck and belly.

They're a songbird and a type of Finch. All the Redpolls usually live in the Arctic or just south of the Arctic. No other songbird is as good as Redpolls at staying alive when it gets very cold. They can survive when the temperature goes down to -65 degrees F. or -54 degrees C. That's too cold for humans and most animals to survive.

To deal with winter cold, Redpolls are clever. They build snow tunnels that can be 1 foot or 30 centimetres long. They shelter inside their tunnels, insulated by the snow.

Another smart thing Redpolls can do is shake birch tree catkins, then fly to the ground to eat the seeds.

They're big eaters! To survive winter weather, they need to eat almost half their body mass every day in seeds. Body mass is how big a body is, or how much space it takes up.

Redpolls are a small bird that likes to take long trips. One that was banded in Alaska later turned up on the U.S. East Coast. Another was spotted in Belgium, Europe and, two years later, was found in China!

There are tens of millions of Redpolls in the world today. At feeders, they're hoping to find black oil sunflower seeds or nyjer (say this: nye-jer) seeds.

Woodpecker

Woodpeckers pound their heads into trees, searching for insects to eat. You'd think all this pounding would give them headaches! Instead, all this drumming is their song. It has no melody, just beats!

If humans pecked wood like Woodpeckers do, we'd probably knock ourselves out. They don't because they have an extra-strong brain case and their skull is thicker, for their size, than other animals' or humans' sculls. They also have extra muscles behind their beaks that help cushion their brains from all that tree-knocking.

Hairy Woodpecker parents take turns sitting on their eggs to incubate them until they hatch.

There are 28 species of Woodpeckers in United States, Mexico and Canada. Some migrate, but many stay year-round. The ones you are most likely to see in your backyard are the Downy Woodpecker, Red-bellied Woodpecker and Hairy Woodpecker.

Downy Woodpeckers are the smallest Woodpeckers in North America. There are more of them than any other type of Woodpecker, so they're the one you're most likely to see. They live everywhere except the American Southwest, where it is too dry for them. They eat mostly insects in summer, but in winter come looking for seeds, berries and suet.

Hairy Woodpeckers look like the big brother of Downy Woodpeckers. They're exactly alike except Hairy Woodpeckers are about 2 ½ inches, or 6.3 centimetres longer. Hairy Woodpeckers also have a thicker body and longer bill than Downy Woodpeckers. They both like to be in the forest but will come to backyards with large trees.

In winter, they like seeds, berries, nuts and suet. In the East, they like to nest in deciduous trees. Deciduous trees are the ones that lose all their leaves in winter. In the West, they prefer aspens or dead evergreen trees for their nests. Females sit on their eggs during the day, but at night males keep the babies warm while their mother sleeps.

Red-bellied Woodpeckers live in all of the Eastern half of United States and only in Southern Ontario in Canada. They usually live in forests and especially near rivers or marshes. They tuck seeds in small openings in the bark of trees to eat in winter. In the North they have only one family per summer but can

The Tufted Titmouse and its Titmouse cousins are shy birds but they can be tempted to come to backyard feeders for chunks of peanuts.

have two or three in Southern United States. They nest in nesting boxes or in holes in tree trunks.

Tufted Titmouse

This little bird isn't related to mice. They got their name because in England the word "mouse" meant "small bird" long ago.

Common in Eastern United States all year, they come to feeders in winter looking for seeds, suet and broken-up peanuts. You might even be able to coax a Tufted Titmouse to come to your hand for food.

In Western United States there are some Tufted Titmouse cousins. They're the Juniper Titmouse, Oak Titmouse and Black-Crested Titmouse. All of these Westerners are a bit shy about people but will come to feeders.

In summer, they eat bugs and especially like wasps, spiders and snails. In summer, they like to line their nests with animal fur or human hair. If there's a bird on your head pulling your hair, it might be a Titmouse!

American Robin

Usually, when animals have the same name, they're the same, or at least in the same family. That's not true for Robins. American Robins, English or European Robins and Australian Robins are completely different birds.

Here's how this happened. When English and European settlers got to their new homes in what they called The New World, they were homesick. They missed many things, including the plants, flowers and birds they knew and loved back home. It helped cheer them up to give the names of their favourites to the new plants and birds they found in Canada, United States, Australia and New Zealand.

This is why English and European Robins are small and American Robins are much larger. The English or European Robins and American Robins are red and brown. The Australian Robins look completely different. The only thing they share is the name "Robin" and that they're all songbirds.

All these birds are called Robins, but only the one top right, the American Robin, lives in North America. Top left is the English Robin. It nests in Britain and Europe and migrates to parts of Asia and Africa. Bottom left is the Flame Robin, a songbird that lives in Eastern Australia and Tasmania. Bottom right is the Eastern Yellow Robin of Australia.

American Robins are a type of Thrush. There are seven sub-species of American Robins in North America. They each look only a little bit different than the others. American Robins live almost everywhere in Canada, United States including Alaska and most of Mexico.

Even though many people think that spotting a Robin is a sign of Spring, American Robins don't always

American Robins aren't the only birds that can have blue eggs, but American Robin eggs are the bluest in the bird world. Other North American birds that can have blue eggs are Blackbirds, Starlings, Magpies, House Finches, Eastern Bluebirds, Catbirds and Blue Jays.

migrate. Some stay all through Winter in places where it snows. In summer, they eat earthworms in the morning, but prefer to eat fruit in the afternoon.

Robins are the first to sing in the Dawn Chorus on summer mornings. Their morning song is the sweetest and longest. Later in the day, their song has more whistles.

Robins don't eat seeds, but they will come to feeders looking for mealworms, jelly or berries. In summer and autumn, they visit backyards with chokecherries, mountain ash, or staghorn sumac to eat the fruit from the trees. They have very good eyesight. They can stand still and wait for the slightest movement in the ground that means there's an earthworm not far under their feet.

Robins' eggs are usually blue. This is because the female covers the eggshells with biliverdin, which might fight off diseases and makes them look blue. When the eggs are very blue it means the female Robin is very healthy. Ornithologists have discovered that male Robins will work harder to feed the babies who are born from very blue eggs.

Chickadee

Chickadees are small, fast and fearless. Nothing can stand between them and getting a seed or a morsel of suet from a feeder! They're usually the first ones to notice when you've just filled your feeders. They have almost no fear of humans, unlike many larger but slower birds.

Chickadees don't migrate. They live year-round almost everywhere in Canada and in Alaska and the Northern half of United States. They're small songbirds known for being very curious about everything. Black-capped Chickadees, the most common type, hide seeds to eat in winter. A Chickadee can remember where there are hundreds of hiding spots with their seeds even months after they placed them there.

Here's how some small birds, including Chickadees and Kinglets, have changed to survive winter cold. They're able to make their own body temperature drop and enter a state of torpor when they sit still and fluff up their feathers to stay warm. They don't need

Chickadees have an incredible memory for the thousands of places they've stored one or two seeds to eat when winter comes.

to wake up to eat. Torpor is something like hibernation, but just for several hours, for example during a storm or the coldest nights.

Chickadees especially like birch and alder trees. They dislike evergreen trees. In summer, they eat insects and berries.

Every Autumn, the memory part of a Chickadee's brain grows one-third bigger to help it remember where it stored seeds all summer. In spring, Chickadees' brains go back to the normal size. No other animal is known to do this.

Northern Flickers are one of the larger types of Woodpeckers.

Northern Flicker

Northern Flickers are a type of Woodpecker that likes to eat ants. They live in Canada, United States, Cuba, Mexico and Central America.

Northern Flickers look for winter food at feeders. Their favourites are suet, corn, sunflower seeds, grapes and apples. You can also help them in summer by putting a nest box in a shady spot on a tree trunk that's at least 10 feet or 3 meters away from other trees.

An odd fact about Northern Flickers is they are the only type of Woodpecker that has brown feathers. Another fact is their strange way of flying. They flap their wings to get high in the air, then stop. They drift

This Mourning Dove has fluffed up to keep warm and locked its legs and feet, allowing it to sleep standing up.

back towards the ground and then start flapping again.

Mourning Dove

Mourning Doves live everywhere in United States and Mexico and in the southern half of Canada. There are none in the Far North, including Alaska.

When you hear their calls, you might think there is a nearby owl hooting. But if it's daytime, what you're probably hearing is a Mourning Dove. Though they sound like owls, they look like pigeons.

Morning Doves are fast fliers among the Backyard Birds. They can cruise at 40 miles per hour, or 64 kilometres per hour. When chased by a predator, they can reach 55 miles per hour, or 88 kilometres per hour. That's twice as fast as most birds can fly!

They are big family birds, having 5 or 6 sets of babies each spring and summer!

Sometimes they eat snails and insects, but they like seeds. They like feeder seeds and prefer to eat the ones that fall to the ground, rather than landing on feeders.

Western Bluebird and Eastern Bluebird

There are lots of birds in North America that are blue or partly blue, but only two are called Bluebirds. That's the Eastern Bluebird and the Western Bluebird.

The males of these two related birds look almost the same. They both are mostly blue, with an orange-brown throat and belly. Females look like the males except instead of blue, they are gray.

They live in Southern Canada, all of United States, most of Mexico and some places in Central America. The ones that spend their summers in more northern places migrate to avoid winter.

Left photo is the Western Bluebird. The photo at the right is the Eastern Bluebird with the female on the left and the male on the right.

The dividing line between the Eastern and Western Bluebirds is the Rocky Mountains. They are social birds and will come to your backyard if you put up nesting boxes. They aren't interested in feeders unless you put out some mealworms.

Males sing with their beaks closed. During mating season, they might sing 1,000 songs to attract a female. They can have two, three or even four nests and families each Spring and Summer.

Bird Fun Fact:
Robins normally eat earthworms, insects and berries. They don't like seeds, but they really like fruitcake and coconut cake!

Pine Siskins squabble over seeds at a tube feeder.

Pine Siskin

The Pine Siskin usually lives in Canada, Alaska and Northern United States, though it sometimes travels as far south as Northern Mexico.

Pine Siskins can survive in very cold winters, though some migrate. When they do, they join flocks of Goldfinches and Redpolls. They are very fond of nyjer seeds.

In summer, they eat aphids, grubs and spiders.

Backyard Bird Fun Fact:
When birds' hearing is damaged, they have an ability no other animal or human has. Birds are able to repair their hearing.

Above, a male Evening Grosbeak and below, a Pine Grosbeak.

A male Rose-breasted Grosbeak. They like seeds and fruit.

Grossbeak

Grossbeaks are a type of Finch. Sadly, they are becoming rarer in United States and Canada. This means there are fewer of them than there used to be.

There are several types, in several colors. The male Rose-Breasted Grossbeak is black and white with a red breast. The females are brown and cream.

The Blue Grossbeak only lives in Southern United States. Only the males are blue. The females are brown. The Black-Headed Grossbeak lives only in the Western United States. The males are orange and black. The Pine Grossbeak is a spectacular bird that has only a small winter range in Western U.S., but sometimes wanders East. They also live in Alaska.

Pine Grossbeaks live and nest almost everywhere in Canada. The male is pinkish-red, with gray wings.

In the Eastern U.S. and Canada, you might see Evening Grosbeaks at feeders looking for sunflower seeds. The males are a bright golden yellow, black and white.

Canada Jay

Canada Jays, also called Whiskey Jacks, are a songbird that prefers cold weather. They live almost everywhere in Canada and also in Alaska and parts of Northwestern United States. Though they could wait for the warmer months of springtime to have their families like other birds do, Canada Jays always have their babies in winter.

They're very curious and aren't picky eaters. Canada Jays will eat almost anything. They like berries, but also eat baby bats. They've been seen landing on a moose's back to eat the ticks that are biting it.

Canada Jays used to be called Gray Jays.

Like their cousins the Blue Jays, they collect food and save it for winter. They use their sticky saliva to glue the food to high tree branches. They also have very thick feathers that they can fluff up to keep warm.

This is how they can survive all year in very cold places where most birds have migrated away from to avoid the cold.

Backyard Bird Fun Fact:
The scientists who study birds are called ornithologists [say this: or-nith-all-oh-jists]. People who have a hobby of being interested in birds are called birders or birdwatchers.

Brown Thrashers got their name for their habit of thrashing through leaves looking for bugs.

Brown Thrasher

This little brown and tan bird has a surprising talent for singing! Males can sing more than 1,100 songs!

They can also do something no human or other animal can do. Brown Thrashers can sing TWO tones, or notes, at the same time!

This is possible because they have a double vocal organ. That's the part of your throat that makes sound.

In summer, they use their tails like a broom, sweeping up leaves to find beetles.

They also thrash, or rake through leaves with their powerful beaks. That's how they got their name.

They live in Canada and United States. Some migrate to warmer parts of U.S. in winter.

Backyard Bird Fun Fact:

All animals, including birds, have a range. That's all the places they usually live.

Some birds live in the same place all year. Others migrate to find places that are warmer, cooler, or have more food or fewer predators.

Predators are the other birds or animals that eat them.

Stellar's Jays will come to feeders with seeds, nuts, berries or suet.

Stellar's Jay

If you live in Eastern United States or Eastern Canada and take a road trip west, as you drive into the Rocky Mountains you will notice that there are no more Blue Jays. Instead, there are Stellar's Jays. Stellar's Jays have blue bodies and black heads with an impressive black crest, like a crown on their head. Like all Jays, they like to be where people are, in backyards, parks, and at campsites.

They are a clever bird, related to Crows and Magpies.

Stellar's Jays have their own call but can also growl and they like to mimic sounds other birds and animals make, like the shrieks of hawks. They like suet, seeds, nuts and berries.

Only the male Ruby-Crowned Kinglet has a tiny red feather crown, and it's usually hidden.

Ruby-Crowned Kinglet

This little bird is one of the smallest songbirds in the world. They live in most of United States including Alaska and almost all of Canada and Mexico. They can fly so fast you barely see them!

Ruby-Crowned Kinglets live in small groups, usually with Chickadees.

They eat insects in summer but in winter will visit feeders for small seeds and suet.

Black Phoebes are a Southwestern U.S. bird, but sometimes travel East.

Black Phoebe

This bird lives in California, some parts of the American Southwest, Mexico, Central America and Western South America. They sometimes travel East. One was spotted in Florida recently by surprised birdwatchers, and another turned up in Minnesota!

Black Phoebes won't come to feeders, but they might hunt for insects in your backyard. A female might even build her mud nest in your yard if you have a pond or birdbath.

This is a Spotted Towhee. They live in Western United States and Western Canada. Eastern Towhees look almost the same, but they live in Eastern Canada and Eastern United States. These two sometimes meet, and mate, in the American Midwest.

Towhee

Spotted Towhees and the bird that looks almost the same, the Eastern Towhees are songbirds and a type of Sparrow. They're people shy. A strange fact about them is they have red eyes.

There is also a California Towhee that is entirely gray. Towhees don't like tube feeders, but they do like tray feeders or eating seeds off the ground. They also like suet and peanut pieces.

Male American Goldfinch, left, with some Sparrow friends.

American Goldfinch

Male American Goldfinches are bright yellow with a black cap and black and white wings in the Spring, which is mating season. For the rest of the year, their main color changes to greenish brown. Females look like the winter Goldfinches all year. American Goldfinches live in the southern half of Canada, all of United States except Alaska, and Eastern Mexico.

They will come to tube feeders, especially when they're filled with nyjer seeds. Nyjer seeds are the tiny black seeds of Guizotia plants. Guizotia is a herb with yellow flowers that grows in Africa and India.

One unusual thing about American Goldfinches is that they moult, or lose their old feathers and grow new

Wrens are native to North America and have now spread around the world. The bird on the right is a House Wren. On the left, a Carolina Wren.

ones, two times a year. Other types of birds usually only do this once a year.

Goldfinches are late nesters. They wait until June or July to build their nests and start their families. That's when milkweed and thistle plants produce their seeds, the favourite food of Goldfinches.

Wren

There are 18 types of Wrens in the world. Nine of them live in United States and there are eight types of Wrens in Canada. Wrens live everywhere in Mexico and Central America and almost everywhere in South America. They would love to find a brush pile of branches in your back yard, a great place for insect-hunting!

This spectacular bird is a male Painted Bunting.

Wrens are happy to use an old boot, can or even a box as a nest. They make their nests in trees or nesting boxes, where they also put some helpful spiders to work, eating the mites that attack baby wrens.

Male Wrens start building several nests, then show them to their mates. Females choose the nest they like and complete it by adding a soft lining. Wrens are one of the few North American songbirds that don't migrate.

Painted Bunting

This bird is so colorful, you might think it's a small parrot. It's not. Only the male Painted Buntings have these jewel colors, and only after they are two years old.

Females look nothing like the males. They are all one color, green. Painted Buntings summer in Southeastern United States and along the Atlantic coast. In some years, they may go as far north as New England and into New Brunswick, Canada. They winter in South Florida, Cuba and Mexico.

Once, these colorful birds were kept as pets, but that is now against the law. In Spring they eat insects but eat seeds all year. They're a shy bird, but sometimes will come to feeders.

Males have a red ring around their eyes. Females have a gray ring around their eyes.

Gray Catbird

Gray Catbirds live year-round along the Atlantic coast of United States. They summer in Canada and all of United States except California and the Southwest.

Catbirds are named for their call that sounds like a cat's meow, but they can also mimic tree frogs, other birds and the sounds of machinery! They eat insects, earthworms and berries. One thing they like to eat is poison ivy!

It can be hard to spot them because they usually only sing when they're well-hidden at the center of a dense

Catbirds sing very long songs.

shrub or tree. Most songbirds have short songs that they repeat several times. Gray Catbirds only sing their song once, but it's a very long song, lasting 10 minutes! Males sing it loudly, to announce their territory and tell other male Gray Catbirds to scram. Females sing the same song, very softly, back to their mates.

Backyard Bird Fun Fact:

Birds have good hearing. You can't see their ears because they are just small openings on their heads below and behind their eyes and hidden by their feathers.

Scarlet Tanagers make long migration journeys each year.

Scarlet Tanager

There are many types of Tanagers, but only six live in North America. This one, the brilliant Scarlet Tanager, lives in the Northeast and Central United States and in Southern Canada as far west as Manitoba in summer. They spend their winters in South America.

They will come to platform feeders, looking for oranges that are cut in half, raisins or mealworms.

You can buy mealworms at pet stores or online.

California Scrub Jays are smart birds that know how to plan for the future!

California Scrub Jay

The California Scrub Jay is a Blue Jay cousin that only lives in Southern British Columbia, Canada, all along the Pacific coast in United States and down to the tip of Baja California in Mexico.

Scrub Jays are the only animal that can plan ahead. They will think about what they'd like to eat for tomorrow's breakfast, find it and hide it close to where they spend the night.

California Scrub Jays visit feeders looking for peanut pieces and sunflower seeds. There is also a Florida Scrub Jay that looks almost the same except it has more white on its back and a white cap.

Baltimore Orioles build hanging nests that are shaped like sacks.

Like Crows and other types of Jays, they steal food from other birds and hide their food in caches, sort of like a bird pantry.

Baltimore Oriole

Baltimore Orioles build carefully woven nests using grass, grapevines and horsehair. They're a cousin of blackbirds.

They didn't get their name from the city of Baltimore, Maryland in United States, but because of their bright orange and black feathers. Those are the same colors as the heraldic crest of the noble Baltimore family of England. The American city was named after Lord Baltimore, a founder of the State of Maryland.

Baltimore Orioles live in Southern Canada from the Atlantic Ocean to the Rockies and in almost all of the Eastern half of United States, parts of Mexico and Central America.

The sound they make is a sharp whistle. They prefer to live near marshes or ponds. They eat caterpillars and flower nectar, but don't like seeds. You can attract them to your feeder if you put out an orange cut in half.

They also like fruit jelly and sugar water. If you plant trumpet vines, crab apples or raspberries in your yard, you'll likely see some Baltimore Oriole visitors.

Males don't get their bright orange feathers until they are two years old. In most birds, the female is not as bright a color as the male. This is to help her hide from predators, especially when she's sitting on her nest. An odd fact about Baltimore Orioles is that females can also have orange feathers. The older the females get, the more orange their feathers get!

Backyard Bird Fun Fact:
Jays, Crows, Ravens and Magpies are all members of the Corvid family of birds. Corvids are known for being smart tricksters who can mimic other birds' calls and songs.

It's easy to mistake a Crow, on the left, for a Raven, on the right. One way to tell the difference is Ravens are larger, with a longer beak.

Crow

Most people aren't too happy to see Crows. Maybe it's because of their noisy caw-caw-caw calls or that they're messy. Crows are also thieves. Some people think they're a sign of bad luck, but that's just superstition.

The truth is that Crows can do some amazing things! They're a member of the smart Corvid family of birds that also includes all the Jays, Magpies and Rooks.

Scientists who study the brainpower of birds say that Crows are as smart as a kid who is seven years old!

Here are some smart things we know Crows can do. They are able to solve problems like how to crack open a walnut to get the food inside. They wait at an intersection and watch the traffic. When the lights turn red, they put their walnut out on the road and get out of the way. When the light turns green, they know chances are good a car will run over the nut and not them. They sit at the side of the road, watching. As soon as the traffic light changes again, they grab their crushed nut prize before any other bird can.

Crows are able to think and plan how to solve a problem. When their idea doesn't quite work out, they will try something different. That's way smarter than almost any other bird except Parrots.

Crows have been seen making stick tools to get food. They can and do steal human food, even drinking coffee or beer when they can get it. They are brilliant mimics and can make almost any sound they hear, like dogs barking. It is wrong to think they only steal bright, shiny objects. They steal anything they think they want. Sometimes, these things become gifts to people they like! They will attack people they don't like.

Crows are able to recognize people's faces. Dogs, monkeys, sheep, octopuses and pigeons can also recognize and remember people. Something these other animals don't do that Crows do is teach their babies about which people to like and trust, and who to avoid or attack.

Crows can recognize human feelings and emotions! There are some animals we know can do this, like Chimpanzees, Dogs and Horses, but the only birds that can are Crows. Like dogs, Crows can learn the names of objects.

Backyard Bird Fun Fact:
Crows are the world's smartest bird.

This is a male Dark-eyed Junco.

Crows live in large, matrilineal families. Matrilineal means families run by the mothers. Crow daughters from last year, or maybe the year before return in Summer to help their mothers raise the new babies. They will feed their mother while she sits on the eggs. When a family member dies, Crows gather to mourn, just like human funerals. It seems that Crows are more like us than we ever imagined.

Dark-eyed Junco

Juncos are a small, shy ground bird. You'll see them hopping along and chirping as they search for insects and seeds. They live almost everywhere in Canada and United States as well as Northern Mexico.

There are 15 known types of Juncos in North America. They're all the same bird but with slightly different colors. Males of the most commonly-seen type in Eastern United States and Canada are dark gray with a white belly. Females look the same, but with browner feathers. Out West, the Oregon Dark-eyed Junco is the one you're most likely to see. The male has a black head and a copper, tan, cream and black body and wings.

They are so fond of coming to feeders in winter that in many places Juncos are known as "snowbirds." Their favourite feeder is a platform. Their favourite winter food is white millet, also called proso millet. They also like berries.

Here's something strange about Juncos. Usually, birds only mate with their own type. That's not true for some Juncos. Even though they look very different, Juncos and White-Throated Sparrows sometimes mate, creating babies that don't have a name. Maybe they're Sparrcos? Or Junrows?

Indigo Bunting

Indigo is a shade of bright blue, like the sky on a sunny summer day. Male Indigo Buntings are entirely this blue. The females are sandy brown. They eat insects and seeds and love nyjer seeds.

Indigo Buntings are a small bird, about the size of a sparrow. They live everywhere in Southern Canada, in all of United States and Mexico and all the way south to Northern South America.

Males learn their songs from nearby male Indigo Buntings but not from their own fathers. Another odd

Indigo Buntings navigate by the stars when they migrate.

thing about them is that all the Indigo Buntings in one area sing the same song. Indigo Buntings that live somewhere else sing a different song, even when that's not very far away!

Like some other songbirds, their songs can change over time as some birds make small changes and every other male Indigo Bunting in their neighbourhood copies them.

Indigo Buntings migrate by flying at night, using the stars to navigate. Navigate means figure out where you're going, usually by using a map. Incredibly, Indigo Buntings have a sort of brain clock that tells

Magpies can mimic anything they hear including the songs of other birds.

them where they are compared to the stars' positions in the sky.

The Earth rotates at night, just like it does in daytime. This means the stars appear to move through the sky. So Earth, birds and stars are all moving, but even so, Indigo Buntings know exactly where they are when they're migrating!

Magpie

Magpies live in Western Canada and on the Canadian Prairies, the American Plains and most of Mid-western and Western United States and Alaska. One way you can spot a Magpie is their very long tail. They eat insects and roadkill as well as small animals like mice. They visit backyards looking for bugs, seeds or suet.

Native peoples of North America knew this bird well because it would follow them in summer, even coming into tents to steal scraps of bison meat. Magpies also pick ticks off the backs of deer, elk, moose and bison, sometimes storing them to eat later.

Magpies build huge nests that look like big twiggy bushel baskets stuck up in the trees.

European Starlings

European Starlings, or Common Starlings, are related to Mynah birds. Like them, male Starlings have a gift for mimicking other birds.

Starlings are another foreign bird that has thrived in Canada and United States. How they got here is a strange story. It seems that back in the 1890s Eugene Schieffelin, a pharmacist who was a devoted birdwatcher, thought it would be a great idea to have all 64 birds mentioned in Shakespeare's poems and plays living in New York City's Central Park. Most city people didn't have back yards. This way, he thought, they could still enjoy seeing all these wonderful birds at the park.

To help make this happen, Mr. Schieffelin and his friends brought birds from Europe, Africa and Asia, including 100 Starlings. They set all these foreign birds free in the park. Since then, Starlings have thrived. They've spread to almost everywhere in

Mother Starling feeding a hungry chick.

Canada and United States as well as the Northern half of Mexico.

This was very good news for the Starlings but not so good for North American native birds. The Starlings take the food and nesting places other birds depend on. They also invade nests of other birds, especially Bluebirds and Owls, killing their babies.

During migration in Autumn, Starlings tend to travel in huge flocks, called a murmuration of Starlings. There can be as many as 50,000 birds in one flock! And they'd all just love to hang out at your house, emptying feeders in just minutes and pooping on anything they leave behind. If you're rather not see any backyard Starlings, put out food to attract

Woodpeckers and Blue Jays, the only birds Starlings seem to be afraid of.

Most people think Starlings are pests, but there's one magical thing they can do. In Autumn, Starling flocks fly close together, all whirling in the air and changing direction very suddenly, like a dance in the air. It's as if they're all one large animal, with one brain, rather than thousands of animals.

For centuries, people have wondered about how Starlings can do this. Scientists have studied Starling murmuration [say this: mer-mer-ray-shun]. We still can't explain how so many birds in a huge flock know which way to turn at <u>exactly</u> the same instant. Starling murmuration is still a mystery of the natural world! Perhaps one day bird scientists will discover the Starlings' secret!

Hummingbirds

Hummingbirds are the only birds who can fly in every direction. They can even fly upside down! They can do this because they have the strength to get flight power from both flapping their wings down but also for the up-flap of their wings. Every other bird moves through the air with the power of their wing down-strokes only.

Another thing only a few birds can do, but Hummingbirds do it best, is hover mid-air, like a helicopter. They do this by holding their bodies straight up and flapping their wings back and forth in a figure-8 shape in the air. They're flapping about 50

This is a female Ruby-throated Hummingbird. Their eggs are only as big as a jelly bean!

times every second. That's so fast it's just a blur to us.

Hummingbirds can perch, but they can't walk or run. Towards the end of Summer and early in Autumn they must eat a lot to store up the energy to migrate. That's why it's important to put out sugar nectar feeders in your backyard until October.

Hummingbirds are known to cross the Gulf of Mexico, a distance of 600 miles or more, which is 966 kilometres, to get to their winter homes in Mexico and Central America. They do this by flying non-stop! They always migrate during daylight and stop to eat and sleep at night. Their migration journeys usually last two or three weeks.

This is a male Purple Finch. They look a lot like House Finches.

There are 20 types of Hummingbirds in United States, but only a few species spend their summers in Canada. If you want to see a lot of different Hummingbirds, you might want to go for a vacation in Mexico. There are 58 Hummingbird species in Mexico.

Here are Hummingbird havens in United States you might also decide to visit:

- Southeastern Arizona Bird Observatory, Bisbee, Arizona
- Davis Mountain State Park, Fort Davis, Texas
- Rio Grande Valley, Texas
- Cabrillo National Monument, California

Purple Finch

The Purple Finch is a type of Finch, but it isn't purple. The males are pinkish-red with mostly brown wings. Females are all brown and look like sparrows.

Red-winged Blackbirds have a loud, piercing whistle.

They live along the West coast and in all of the
Eastern half of United States and across Canada from
British Columbia to Newfoundland. You'll often see
them, and their close cousins the House Finches, in
city parks as well as back yards. They're frequent
feeder guests!

Red-winged Blackbird

Male Red-winged Blackbirds have a bright flash of red
and yellow on their wings. Females are brown, gray
and black. They prefer to spend most of their time and
build their nest in marshes close to water. They will
come to backyards looking for insects and seeds.

They gather with other Red-winged Blackbirds to roost together and sleep at night. Birds at the edge of the flock stay awake to stand guard.

Some birds mate for life. Others stay with their mate for just one summer. But male Red-winged Blackbirds are the bad boys of the bird world. They can have as many as 15 mates, fathering 15 families, in just one summer! This keeps the male very busy from May to August, defending his territory and all those nests from predators.

Waxwing

Cedar Waxwings spend summers in Canada and Northern United States or year-round everywhere in the U.S. except Alaska or Mexico. Sometimes they venture further South, to Costa Rica and Panama. Their very close cousins, who look almost exactly the same, are Bohemian Waxwings. They live almost everywhere in Canada and the Northern half of United States plus Alaska.

Backyard Bird Fun Fact:
Birds are able to hear the smallest changes in another bird's song. When humans were tested by listening to the same songs, they couldn't hear these subtle song changes.

A Bohemian Waxwing foraging for fruit.

Waxwings love fruit. To attract them, put out some raisins, berries or put a fruit and nut bird food mix in your feeders. They'll also come to parks or backyards where there are berry or holly bushes, honeysuckle bushes or vines or crabapple, dogwood, mountain ash or cedar trees.

Backyard Bird Fun Fact:
Almost every year, ornithologists discover five or six new species of birds we did not know about. This is usually in remote places where few people live.

Bird babies need to grow up fast to be ready to migrate or survive colder weather when they're only a few months old. These are baby Rusty Blackbirds with their mother.

Why some backyard birds migrate

Birds go to where they have a better chance to survive and raise their babies. A place that is a bit warmer or has more food or more safe places to rest, sleep and nest or has fewer predators like vultures, hawks, owls and cats is where they want to be.

This changes through the seasons in most places. In the North, colder weather sends many birds South in Autumn. In the South, heat or hurricanes can send them North in Spring.

Left, this Brambling is a type of Finch. Bramblings usually live in Scandinavia, Europe, Central Asia Western Africa. Very rarely, Bramblings get blown off course and turn up in Eastern Canada and Eastern United States. Right, a male Bullfinch. They're not native to North America but do sometimes become accidental tourists to Eastern United States.

For most types of songbirds, the males migrate ahead of the females. They do this to claim their territory, where they sing to warn off competitors and also to attract a mate.

Are there vagrants in your backyard?

Have you ever started to go somewhere, but then for some reason you ended up somewhere completely different? Somehow you just got sidetracked!

Birds know the feeling. Storms can mean they have to take a break from migrating, landing in an unfamiliar place. Winds can blow them far off course. They might end up in a part of the country, or even another country, on another continent. This can be confusing for the birds. It's usually very exciting for the bird lovers who might never have had a chance to see this bird before.

When this happens, the unusual bird visitors are called, "vagrants." Vagrants usually don't stay for long, though they might stop for a while to rest, particularly if they've landed somewhere with plenty of food.

If you'd like to see vagrants, a good place to go would be Newfoundland, Canada in Spring or Autumn. Newfoundland is the furthest-East place in North America. In Spring, 2022 several bird vagrants turned up in Newfoundland that are natives in Iceland, Europe and Russia. They were blown there during their Spring migration in a year of especially strong winds across the North Atlantic. There were several Black-tailed Godwits and Barnacle Geese, a Northern Lapwing, several European Golden Plovers and, rarest of all, a Brambling.

Climate change is bringing more changeable and powerful weather, so it's likely that more vagrants will come to visit our parks and backyards on their long, interrupted journeys to somewhere else. Especially if you live on the East Coast of Canada or United States, there might be vagrants set to thrill birders coming to your yard, or one that's nearby, soon!

This Titmouse seems to dance in the air as it collects berries from a garden vine.

How birds help people

Birds are beautiful, strange, smart and interesting. There are many ways they help people. If there were no birds, the world would be less beautiful and less magical. It might even be true that humans would not survive. This is because, like insects, birds help to pollinate plants and spread their seeds. This means the plants will continue to survive, to feed the world's hungry populations of animals and people.

Birds and climate change

Over the many millions of years birds have lived on earth they have faced climate change many times. In some centuries, the climate was warmer than now. For example, Antarctica was once semi-tropical, something like Northern Florida or the Southern half of Australia is today. In other times, it was much colder. Animals change to be able to survive when our world changes. This is called adaptation [say this: a-dap-tay-shun].

Usually, it takes a long time and many generations for any creature to adapt. Just like us, animals and plants need time to make change slowly. It is much harder, and sometimes not even possible, to make very sudden and big changes.

Right now, our climate is growing warmer.

Backyard birds are adapting to this climate change by changing their range. Range is the total area where they normally live. They are seeking places that have the cooler or milder weather they are used to, or that are less affected by wildfires, flooding, drought and other disasters.

Like us, backyard birds just want to find a place that has fresh air and water, good food and it feels safe so they can live their normal lives.

Backyard Bird Fun Fact:
A Hummingbird's heart beats up to 1,000 times a minute. Normal heartbeat for people is 60 to 100 times per minute.

Every year cats kill millions of wild birds in United States and Canada.

Save the birds!

Today, there are three billion fewer birds in North America than there were 50 years ago. That's a huge number! If you wrote it out, it would look like this: 3,000,000,000.

Though some types of backyard birds, like Starlings, Sparrows and Mourning Doves are thriving, we need to do more to help the many types of birds that are struggling. It's up to us, the people who love birds, to help save them.

Birds fly into windows, or windmills. They're hit by cars, drones or airplanes. They're killed by other animals, especially by pet cats allowed outside.

Birds also die in storms, like hurricanes. Birds have the ability to hear infrasound. That's sounds that humans can't hear. The earth and storms make infrasounds that signal storms are coming. Birds can also sense barometric pressure, which changes before a storm. Even when birds know about a storm and take shelter, they might accidentally fly into a storm, or shelter in a place that isn't safe.

Humans are the cause of many birds' struggles to survive. Hunting, poaching and destroying the places they live means birds have fewer places to find safety. Poaching means stealing the birds, to eat or sell as pets. Wild birds do not want to be pets. They want their wild life.

Some of the things people do to try to protect birds, like put a picture of a flying hawk in a window, don't work. Birds don't understand what glass is. It looks like open air to them, or maybe a reflection off of water. They also don't understand a silhouette of a hawk. It doesn't look like a flying hawk in the way they see their enemy. This is because birds see very differently, in different colours, than we do.

A better way to protect birds from hitting windows is to put screens on the outside of your windows. Draw curtains or blinds shut when you're not in the room.

Backyard Bird Fun Fact:
Magpies know how to play the game hide-and-seek. They are just as good at it as children who are 5 years old!

It will help the birds a lot to keep pet cats indoors. Many millions of birds' lives would be saved if all pet cats were indoor cats. This is also much better for the cats. Cats that are outside can also be hit by cars, attacked by other animals, catch parasites and diseases from wild animals or eat plants that are poison for them. Indoor cats live longer, healthier lives.

Many people doing small things, like feeding birds in winter and protecting them from dangers, can make a huge difference for the backyard birds we love. There are already some happy success stories of birds that were endangered, but today their numbers are growing because people cared enough to try to save them. One of these is the Eastern Bluebird. Not very long ago, they were disappearing. It seemed they might even become extinct, like the Carolina Parakeet. The last Carolina Parakeet died in 1918. It was the only native parakeet in North America.

How to help birds in summer

Just like us, birds need to be able to cool down on days that are too hot.

They need shady places to rest. Plant shrubs and trees to give them shelter from the sun. This will also work to help cool your home. These are some plant that provide shelter and fruit for birds to eat:

Virginia creeper – In winter, Blue Jays, Mockingbirds, Nuthatches and Woodpeckers eat the fruit.

Even a simple plate set in a tree attracts backyard birds like this Red-breasted Nuthatch.

Elderberry – Many songbirds enjoy the red fruit of this tree in winter.

Staghorn Sumac – This shrub gives fruit in autumn and winter to Robins, Catbirds, Cardinals, Chickadees, Thrushes and Starlings.

Give your backyard birds fresh, cool water in a birdbath or a shallow dish, like a plant pot saucer. Put it somewhere that cats or other predators can't reach. In hot weather, empty your bird bath, clean it and refill it once a day.

Birds need help finding food in summer before the plants go to seed. Hummingbirds need sugar nectar in feeders, especially before their favorite flowers bloom and after those flowers are done for the year.

Don't stop feeding in August. All the migrating birds need to eat to fuel up before their long journeys. Birds that don't migrate need to fuel up to prepare for the coming cooler or cold weather.

Make nesting and habitat places for the birds. There are lots of things you can make birdhouses out of. An old teapot hung up sideways, a colander with a roof or a basket can all make good nesting sites for birds. Get creative and have some fun helping the birds!

Helping Backyard Birds in winter

Birds need food, water and shelter year-round. You can make all these easy for birds to find in your backyard.

You could put out fresh water. Birds who can't find water will eat snow, but that uses up precious food energy to heat up the snow in their mouths so they can swallow it.

You can provide shelter. Clean out nesting boxes after the last family has left and place them back in the trees. Plant shelter plants, like evergreen trees and shrubs in your yard.

You can feed the backyard birds. In winter, especially after a snowfall, food is harder to find for birds. Songbirds that don't migrate depend on being able to find enough seeds and fruit to get through the cold season. With insects much harder to find, other backyard birds like Woodpeckers, Orioles, Tanagers and Mourning Doves also need seeds and suet to help them get through winter.

Suet gives birds like this Titmouse the fats they need to survive cold weather.

There are many different kinds of mixes of bird food at the stores. It can be confusing to know which one to buy. A quality brand of black-oil sunflower seeds and suet cakes will attract all of the backyard birds. Mourning doves, Jays, Sparrows and Blackbirds would also like some dried, whole-kernel corn.

The reason black-oil sunflower seeds are so popular at feeders is they are small, with shells that are easy to crack. The nut inside is a high-energy food for birds. It's better to buy a bag of all-sunflower seeds, rather than a seed mix with lots of different seeds and only some sunflower seeds. The reason is most birds will ignore the other seeds. Worse yet, these other seeds can mold, making the birds sick.

Peanut butter is a great choice for backyard birds. So are the seeds from your Halloween pumpkins, squash and melons. Wash the seeds, dry them completely by spreading them out on cookie sheets and store them in a cool, dry place.

What not to feed the birds: Stale bread, because it can also be moldy, making them sick. Table scraps are also a bad idea, because these can attract rats, racoons and other animals you probably don't want as back yard visitors.

How to attract more Backyard Birds to your yard

Once some birds start coming to your feeders, other birds will notice and join them. Usually, the first birds to check out a new feeder are the Chickadees.

You could plant the flowers that birds feed on. These are: coneflowers (they're also called echinacea), sunflowers, asters and black-eyed Susans (also called rudbeckia). More flowers birds like are cornflowers, daisies, and marigolds. Any flower with a trumpet-shape, like petunias, will attract Hummingbirds.

Put out a variety of feeders. The smallest birds generally prefer tube feeders, while larger birds like a platform-style feeder best.

And remember the squirrels and chipmunks. Though there are many feeders sold that promise to be squirrel-proof, squirrels turn out to be smarter than those feeders. They can and will take over any type of bird feeder, scaring the birds away. So, why not give

A Spotted Towhee cools off on a hot summer day. Birds need fresh water year-round to survive.

the squirrels their own feeder in another part of your backyard or school garden or park? At the squirrel feeder you can put out some peanuts in the shells or broken up. That should keep everyone happy and no more squirrel battles!

Backyard Bird Fun Fact:
Robins won't use a nesting box, but they might build their nest on a nesting platform, windowsill or even in a hanging flower planter.

These little American Robins are counting on you to help them survive!

What bird is that?

Wondering what bird that is in your yard? Ornithologists at Cornell University in New York have created two great apps to identify birds and, if you want, keep track of the birds you've seen. There are photos, the songs and sounds birds make and searchable information for more than 8,000 birds to help you identify that unusual bird you've just seen. These apps are free. They are:

- Merlin Bird ID
- eBird

You can find more ways to help the birds, live Birdcams, birder courses and more online at:

- www.allaboutbirds.org

- www.birdscanada.org

There are also birdwatching locations, meet-ups and more – find them at **Birdability, Flock Together, The Feminist Bird Club** and **Birds Canada**, or put your location and "birdwatching" into your search box to find local groups.

Birding is an interest that is the fastest-growing hobby in North America. You'll find plenty of people out there who share your interest in discovering and enjoying the beauty and mysteries of birds!

Thanks for reading!

Jacquelyn

Backyard Bird Fun Fact:

Birds don't have a nose, so how do they breathe? The do it through small holes in their beaks, called nares. They draw air into their air sacs and exhale air from the air sacs to their lungs or out of their bodies.

About the Author

Jacquelyn Elnor Johnson started telling stories to entertain her younger sisters when she was 10. They were a tough audience! By age 15, she was a writing for the local newspaper and had written her first book. She went on to have careers in writing for and editing newspapers and magazines and teaching journalism in United States and Canada.

In 2014, she moved with her family to Nova Scotia, drawn by the opportunity to live near the ocean. A life-long pet lover, she is the bestselling author of 13 books about caring for and enjoying pets and animals, including **I Want A Bearded Dragon** and **The Complete Bearded Dragon Care Book**.

She also writes novels including the Morley Stories series for girls ages 10 to 13.

Find all her books and more at **www.CrimsonHillBooks.com**

PHOTO CREDITS

Thank you to these Pixabay photo artists:

Megan Zopf, Jill Wellington, 165106, Scottslm, Oldiefan, Ray Miller, MD Herren, Dirtdiver38, Zenaga, Hans Toom, Homecare119, Jack Bulmer, Kurt Bouda, Teefarm, Dr. George Wietschorke, Geraldine Rose, Sid Latke, Pen Ash, Daina Krumins, Alan Audet, Susan Killian, Daledbet, Erik Karits, 16081684, Steph McBlack, Miles Moody, I Love Animals, Public Domain Images, GloverBH222, Veronika Andrews, Irene K-s, Sabrina and Stephan Martens, Vincent Simard, Jen Kindell, Diapicard, Alexas Fotos, Logga Wiggler, Daniel Bisett, Israel Alapag, Mabel Amber, Gerhard G., AnjaGh, Bryan Hanson, Shauna Fletcher, Eveline de Bruin, Ralphs Fotos, Anita Stachurski and George B2.

LOVED all these great backyard bird facts?

Want to know even MORE about wild birds? Don't miss **Fun Bird Facts for Kids**! You can find it where you bought this book.

Discover MORE Fun Facts books from Crimson Hill Books:

- **Fun Dog Facts for Kids**
- **Fun Cat Facts for Kids**
- **Fun Leopard Gecko and Bearded Dragon Facts for Kids**
- **Fun Reptile Facts for Kids; Lizards, Turtles, Crocodilians, Snakes and Birds**
- **Fun Pony Facts for Kids**
- **Fun Horse Facts for Kids**
- **Fun Bird Facts for Kids**
- **Fun Backyard Bird Facts for Kids**
- **Fun Insect Facts for Kids**

And Don't Miss:

- **Dinosaur Facts for Kids**
- **T-rex Facts for Kids**

www.ingramcontent.com/pod-product-compliance
Lightning Source LLC
Chambersburg PA
CBHW040857120626
46551CB00001B/56